"*Letter from Paul* was couched in comm
The study and personal commentary on Galatians will be a happy
addition to the 'everyday reader' and the library of every Bible student."
—Rev. James J. Counihan

Letter
FROM
PAUL

TO THE
Church in Galatia...
AND US!

Will God get tired of forgiving me?
If I mess up, am I still saved?
What works for my salvation?
To find answers to these questions and more, read on!

Letter
FROM
PAUL

TO THE
Church in Galatia...
AND US!

Will God get tired of forgiving me?
If I mess up, am I still saved?
What works for my salvation?
To find answers to these questions and more, read on!

MARY WEINS

REDEMPTION PRESS

Published by Redemption Press, PO Box 427, Enumclaw, WA 98022
Toll-free (844) 2REDEEM (273-3336)

Redemption Press is honored to present this title in partnership with the author. The views expressed or implied in this work are those of the author. Redemption Press provides our imprint seal representing design excellence, creative content, and high-quality production.

ISBN 13: 978-1-68314-903-3
ePub ISBN: 978-1-68314-909-5
Kindle ISBN: 978-1-68314-919-4
Library of Congress Catalog Card Number: 2019934500

Acknowledgments

Loving thanks to my sister, Marge Lalich, who edited and helped keep me on track. Thanks for her continual support, encouragement, and comments regarding some of the wording and references contained herein.

Special thanks to my friend and mentor, Pastor James Counihan, for his editing and critiquing skills. Jim has a way of keeping me on track and letting me know when I'm preaching too much without discouraging me in the process. I could not have completed this project without his insight and help.

Thanks to my friend, Ann Counihan, who encouraged and supported me through this process as well.

I would also like to thank my husband, Robert, who read every word, supported me, and encouraged my efforts.

Also, special thanks to the gals in our Bible study group: Linda Hutchinson, Rosalie Paiva, Barbara Kobylinski, Carol Agrifoglio, and Brooke Gross. They encouraged and supported me and have added many of the comments through our Bible studies along the way.

Contents

Welcome

As a preacher's kid, I was brought up in a strict, structured home environment. This upbringing created a harsh view of Christianity and an overwhelming fear of hell, fire, and damnation for me.

It was not until years later that I found a church emphasizing God's love. I read the Word and prayed daily, and began to develop a close, personal relationship with God. But fear kept haunting me until I really got into Galatians and broke it down, verse by verse. The book of Galatians is a key book of the Bible for me because it emphasizes God's love and forgiveness and provides assurance that, even though I mess up at times, God still loves me!

It is my hope and prayer that you, too, can embrace the beautiful message of love and acceptance contained in Galatians and apply it to your life. When we fully submit and trust God for our lives, an overwhelming peace envelops us. We no longer need to fear Him. He is a loving God who provides all our needs and protects, encourages, comforts, and directs us. He is our heavenly Father, our constant companion, and a friend who really does have all the right answers.

Living in a right relationship with God dramatically changes the way we view ourselves and the world. "Therefore, if anyone is in Christ, he is a new creation; old things have passed away; behold, all things have become new" (2 Cor. 5:17).

Written in a down-to-earth, easy-to-read approach, the Bible studies contained in *Letter from Paul* highlight the main points covered in each chapter of Galatians. The Bible is a living entity, and through His Word, God reveals certain things to us at various times in our lives. To fully comprehend the studies, it is essential to read the referenced verses in addition to the ones in each chapter.

The overview provides historical background pertinent to the time, place, and circumstances under which Paul wrote the letter and gives us perspective on Paul's state of mind and the challenges he was facing.

Each chapter begins with a story illustrating the main points to be examined within. The story emphasizes how the critical aspects might be relevant to our lives today. Following the devotional is the Bible study itself. Read the verses noted for each section before beginning the study. Questions and Bible references follow each chapter to enhance your understanding.

Personal Application questions follow the Bible study section. These may help you identify areas of spiritual weakness in your life or could provide the assurance you are seeking. Ask God to reveal these to you and to help you overcome or accept them. After the personal application questions, space is provided for you to write down any points of enlightenment and to pause and reflect upon what you read.

Chapters conclude with Something to Ponder—an idea or question for you to internalize and pray about in your walk with the Lord. These are followed by a prayer you may want to incorporate into your daily life.

It is my personal prayer that you will embrace this Bible study series to develop an intimate relationship with the One who loves you more than you love yourself. God, our Father, is our only hope for salvation, through the death and resurrection of His Son, Jesus Christ.

Overview of the Book of Galatians

During his first missionary journey to Asia Minor, Paul worked with others to build churches in Galatia. It was through his work there that he developed a close relationship with Christians and taught them that salvation is by grace through faith in Jesus Christ, not by works or the law of Moses.

One of Paul's many concerns was to teach the Jewish people that gentiles were just as entitled to salvation as they were. This inclusion of the gentiles into the church was the first cause of controversy that upset the church in its early years—Jews and gentiles did not want to bond together. Paul emphasized how vital it was that people embraced unity in Christ, no matter what their race or ethnic background was.

Arriving back in Antioch from his first missionary trip, Paul received a report that the churches he had started in Galatia had become divided. A group of Judaizers—Jews promoting adherence to the Mosaic law—were teaching the necessity of living under the law as a requirement of the Christian faith, including old covenant rites such as circumcision. Additionally, they suggested that living by grace and freedom alone meant a lawless, reprehensible life. These false teachings had significantly impacted the church in Galatia, and Paul was outraged.

Paul wrote his letter a few months before attending the Jerusalem Council in AD 49. The purpose of the Council was to discuss this particular topic. Paul used a sharp tone in his letter because he felt betrayed that some Christians were listening to the false teachers who had come to Galatia since his ministry there. The Christians accepting these false teachings also made clear their disloyalty to Paul's authority as an apostle.

Paul felt a special bond between himself and this church, as he had personally evangelized them. His letter to the Galatians was a swift and decisive attempt to counter the false teachers' message about living under the law. Paul wanted to be sure the Galatians were on the path of truth and were not being deceived.

The book of Galatians was written to emphasize the deadly dangers of relying on works for salvation. No one is ever granted eternal life based on works. In fact, anyone who lives by such confidence in actions is considered cursed, because no one can live a perfect life and completely obey the law (Gal. 3:10).

Adding works, rituals, or the law to the message of Christianity is a travesty; doing so essentially says that salvation through faith is impossible. Such beliefs are against Christianity. We stand justified before God *only* through faith in Jesus Christ; nothing else will save us.

Paul felt so strongly about the problems in the Galatian church that he took the pen from his scribe and signed his name in large, bold letters.

In the final section of his letter, Paul made clear that justification—an act of grace through faith—would not result in a sinful lifestyle. Christians are freed from bondage to the sinful nature and should naturally desire to glorify God through their righteous behavior.

We walk a fine line. On one hand, we do not want to fall into the legalism the Galatians struggled with, but on the other, we must not live as if anything goes. A Christian's commitment to Christ is based on the gift of grace through faith, but as Paul articulated at the end of

Galatians 2, it also results in a life of walking by the Spirit in love (Gal. 2:20).

Is the fruit of the Spirit evident in your life, or are you self-absorbed and living according to the flesh? Too often we lose ourselves at the extremes, ending in a legalistic attempt to earn our salvation or taking a lighthearted attitude about our sins because grace saves us.

Use Paul's words in Galatians as encouragement to pursue a life of holiness—not in your own strength, but in the knowledge of God's empowering grace for you.

CHAPTER 1

Works vs. God's Saving Grace

For by grace you have been saved through faith, and that not of
yourselves; it is the gift of God, not of works, lest anyone should boast.
Ephesians 2:8–9

Samantha's Story

Sitting with her friend Amy, Samantha confided, "I know I'm supposed to be this good Christian girl. Dad always said I'd better not mess up, because if I sin, I will go to hell. I've tried living by all the rules, but I just can't. I keep messing up. I feel like a complete failure, and I'm scared. I don't want to go to hell.

"There is a war going on inside me. I want to serve God and be a good Christian, but I feel like I'm missing out on all the fun in life. Everyone around me seems to be having so much fun, while I'm miserable. I don't go to parties. I don't drink. I don't mess around. I don't even dance, because that's supposed to be a sin too."

Amy said, "Sam, you're not going to hell if you dance. I can't believe the church would even say that. Hey, we're having a party Friday night. Everyone from the office will be there, so you should come. People say you're standoffish, and some say you're a snob. It would be good for you to get to know them better."

"I don't know. I wouldn't know what to talk about. I'll think about it."

Leaving work on Friday, Samantha thought about her conversation with Amy. *Maybe I should go to show them I'm not a snob. I don't have to drink or dance, but I probably should try to get to know them better so they see I'm friendly.*

Slipping into the party, Sam smiled as she walked through the room and headed for the chair in the corner.

Amy came running over. "Hi, Sam! Glad you could make it. Can I get you a drink?"

"I'll have a Coke."

"Oh, come on. Jim makes a great margarita. One drink won't kill you, and it won't send you to hell either."

I suppose I could sip one and make it last till I leave. Then everyone will realize I'm not a prude. "Okay, I'll try one."

Oh, this tastes pretty good. I'll just nurse it along for a while and then leave.

Fred, the office playboy, came running over. "Hi, Sam. Want to dance?"

I can't believe he asked me to dance. He's dated all the good-looking gals in the office. Why would he ask me to dance? I'm not a fashionista. "No, thank you. My feet are hurting after running around in these high heels all day."

"Oh, come on. Just one little dance."

Is he really interested in me after all the girls he's dated? "Okay, one dance."

I don't know why, but he seems to really like me. I'm not dressed up like the other girls. Maybe he has always been interested in me and just didn't think I would be receptive. Anyway, this is fun!

Flattered by Fred's attention, Sam was captivated by his charm. It didn't take him long to arrange a follow-up date with her.

After that party and a few more dates with Fred, she was hooked. Sam began going to many parties and meeting other guys, and thought she was having fun. She didn't realize that she was changing and drifting farther from God. The downhill slide had begun, and before she realized it, she was in full-blown rebellion to God.

This partying lasted a couple of years, and Samantha got to the point where she no longer cared about going to church, praying, or living a righteous life. Life was all about the next party or the next guy. She failed to realize that she no longer felt good about herself or who she was as a person. Her self-esteem now came from the compliments her new friends provided. It didn't matter that they were lowlifes living on the edge. They were building her up and supposedly putting her on a pedestal because she was such a decent person. In other words, she had not yet sunk to their level of behavior.

One night while cleaning up after a party in her home, she had an awakening. (God was speaking to her.) *No one offered to help me clean up tonight. I bet if I ever needed help or had a real problem, none of them would be there for me. My new friends are here only for the good times.*

God, forgive me. I know I've messed up, but I want to change. Please help me.

Samantha began attending a new church and, for the first time, heard about God's love for her. When she realized God loved her even when she made mistakes, a whole new world opened. Samantha accepted Christ as her Savior and then sought Christian counsel to turn her life around. She started reading Scripture to discern God's guidance for her life.

Losing interest in her friends and the parties, Sam made new friends in the church. Her life took on a new dimension. She now wanted to live a righteous life—not because she had to, but because she knew she had a loving Father who had forgiven her sins and would not hold them against her in the future.

Samantha realized that Christ hadn't just died for the sins of the world; He'd died for her sins personally. God would guide and direct her path and give her peace and joy within. For these reasons, she now wanted to serve Him.

Bible Study: Galatians 1

The book of Galatians teaches us the difference between salvation by works and salvation through faith in Jesus Christ. Salvation is not about obeying all the rules versus having a good time. It is about a personal relationship with our Creator and Savior. He is the only one who can give us real peace and joy within. We cannot obtain salvation by our works; our sinful nature will not allow us to live perfect lives. It is the work of the Holy Spirit within each of us that guides, directs, and empowers us, causing us to want to love and serve God and others instead of continuing with the self-serving lives we once led.

GALATIANS 1:1–10

Paul wrote to rebuke the Christians in Galatia for following the Judaizers who had asserted their authority and gained recognition as religious leaders in the churches he had helped to establish.

These leaders preached the necessity of living by the law of Moses and following their religious customs, such as circumcision and other ceremonies. They asserted that anyone who lived by faith in Jesus Christ alone could easily live a sinful life of debauchery, and that type of Christianity would not save them.

> *Test all things; hold fast what is good.*
> 1 Thessalonians 5:21

In his letter, Paul stated that these religious leaders were Satan's tool and were cursed by God (Gal. 1:8). It is important to note that we are challenged to test everything we are told or see, according to God's Word (1 Thess. 5:19–22).

The Judaizers were making rules that were not biblical, while making light of things God said were wrong. They did not believe in salvation through faith in Jesus Christ alone. The Bible teaches that if we try to live by the law, we are in bondage to the law and are estranged from Christ.

The question arose that, since grace saves us, is it okay to sin? No. We are saved by grace, and we obey in love. Our new nature will cause us to want to live a righteous life. We are free to live as we choose, but we should not use this liberty as an opportunity to sin (Galatians 5:13).

Of course, because of our sinful nature we all slip occasionally—no one can live a perfect life—but we must strive to live lives free from sin. We tend to fool ourselves sometimes, thinking it's just a little white lie. We rationalize, justify, and play mind games with ourselves, but a sin is still a sin (Rom. 2:15).

It is important to ask God to show us our sins and to then ask for forgiveness and turn from them. If we truly repent and turn from our wicked ways, God is faithful and just to forgive us.

> *If we confess our sins, He is faithful and just to forgive us our sins and to cleanse us from all unrighteousness.*
> 1 John 1:9

GALATIANS 1:11–24

Paul emphasizes that he is not a biblical scholar; he received the gospel through a personal revelation from Jesus Christ. God revealed His grace and plan of salvation to Paul while Paul was on the road to Damascus (Acts 9:1–9).

Before his conversion, Paul felt he was righteous before God because he was performing so well in the Jewish faith and observing all the Jewish laws and ceremonies. In his mind, he was the leader of the pack and the world revolved around him. Paul readily admits he had previously persecuted Christians while following in the footsteps of the fathers in the Jewish faith. When Christ encountered him on the road to Damascus, Paul immediately left Judaism behind and followed Christ. Paul then spent three years learning about salvation through faith in Jesus Christ before joining Peter and James—the Lord's brother—in Jerusalem (Gal. 1:18–20). From there Paul went to Syria and Cilicia to preach the gospel. Paul no longer lived to empower himself; he lived solely to glorify Jesus Christ.

The Christians in Judea were amazed when they saw Paul again because they knew of his background, and they praised God for the transformation that had taken place in his life.

Study Questions

GALATIANS 1:1–10

Who wrote the book of Galatians?

_____

_____

What was the purpose of his letter? (vv. 6–8)

_____

_____

How did the religious leaders in Galatia distort God's Word? (v. 1)

_____

_____

What happens to people who pervert the Word of God? (v. 9)

_____

_____

_____

Should we take at face value everything a religious leader or pastor says? (vs. 1:6-10)

_____

_____

_____

GALATIANS 1:11–24

Was Paul looking for the real gospel while persecuting the Christians? (vv. 3–14)

_____

_____

Was Paul a religious scholar before he began preaching the gospel of Christ? (vv. 16–21)

_____

_____

How quickly did Paul leave his Jewish traditions behind once God's grace was revealed to him? (v. 16)

_____

_____

_____

How did he prepare himself to preach? (vv. 17–21)

_____

_____

How did the Galatians receive him? (vv. 23–24)

_____

_____

Personal Application

Before answering the following questions, it would be wise to go to God in prayer. Ask Him to reveal any spiritual weaknesses you may be unaware of, any new insights He would have you glean, or any assurances that would enhance your understanding and walk with Him.

"And do not be conformed to this world, but be transformed by the renewing of your mind, that you may prove what is that good and acceptable and perfect will of God" (Rom. 12:2).

Have you ever felt you weren't good enough to receive God's grace? (Phil. 1:6)

_____

_____

Do you believe God will forgive your sins? (1 John 2:2)

_____

_____

_____

Under what circumstances do you believe He will forgive? (Acts 3:19)

_____

_____

Are you living under grace or under the law?

_____

_____

Something to Ponder

If I am living under grace, my new nature will be under the influence and control of the Spirit of God, and I will want to glorify God by living a Christ-centered life!

PRAYER

Thank You, Lord, for providing me with Your Word and Your Holy Spirit. Help me to stay focused on You and Your Word, and to trust only in You. Direct my path daily so I will live to glorify You and be a light unto the world.

Reflections

Use the space provided below to record your reflections on the lesson just completed. Think about the study and all the questions—including the personal application—and record anything that stood out, provided enlightenment, reduced your fears, or enriched your relationship with God.

CHAPTER 2

Beware! False Prophets

Beloved, do not believe every spirit, but test the spirits, whether they are of God; because many false prophets have gone out into the world.
1 John 4:1

Tony's Story

Tony slumped over his crumpled shopping bag full of clothes. *How did I get here? I had everything going for me—a good job, a girlfriend who adored me. What happened?*

"What's up, Tony?" Rusty clomped through the mud and sat down next to him.

"Not much. There doesn't seem to be much work available. Sure wish I could get a job. I'm tired of livin' on the streets." *I wish I had a beer about now.*

"Some guys were just over at the church looking for workers to work on the yard at the mill. They're trying to clean it up and restore the building. They offered fifteen dollars an hour. You interested?"

"Yeah, you bet. I could use the money."

"Good. They're a great outfit to work for. I'll give you a ride over. Hop in."

At the job site, Rusty jumped out of the truck and yelled to the foreman, "Hey, Tom, Tony here is a great worker and could use a job."

"Are you interested in some hard labor? I need people to rototill the yard and generally clean this place up."

"You got it. Where do you want me to start?" asked Tony.

"I need this whole yard dug up except for the hedges. Nick will show you around."

This job will take a few days. Maybe I can do it good enough so they will hire me on permanently.

A crew of about fifteen guys was working in the yard and on the building. Everyone seemed to be glad for the work. Hard times had fallen on the town since the mill had closed.

After work, Rusty came up to Tony. "Nice job today. Some of the guys are going to Nick's place for a barbecue. Want to join us?"

"That would be great." *I haven't had much to eat for the past few days.*

It seemed to be a friendly bunch (except for Nick's wife), and the food was excellent. Tony had a great time playing ball and hanging out with the guys. It was nice to feel a part of the group.

"Hey, Rusty, want a beer?"

"No thanks. I'll stick with the iced tea." Even though he would have enjoyed a beer, he knew better than to tempt Tony, who had a problem with booze.

Nick then called out to Tony. "Hey, Tony, you want one?"

"No thanks. I'll stick with tea too." *They all know I'm a drunk; I've got to prove I can live without it. I need this job.*

Tony worked very hard the next few weeks, keeping his nose to the grindstone. Rusty continued to befriend him.

"Tony, they're having a potluck after church on Sunday. Want to come? I can pick you up for church, and we can go to the potluck after. The food is always great, and lots of it."

"Sure. Sounds good." *I'd better get some decent clothes to wear.*

On Sunday Rusty picked Tony up on the corner by the motel where Tony was staying. When they arrived at church, eyebrows raised, especially those of Nick's holier-than-thou wife.

She thought, *What is he doing here? This church is supposed to be a Christian fellowship. We don't need the homeless hanging around here.*

Choosing to ignore the arrogance, Rusty introduced Tony to a few of the parishioners. Most everyone seemed friendly.

After the service they enjoyed all the food and fellowship, and Tony felt accepted by most everyone.

He then started attending church regularly. It felt good to be accepted in society again. Gradually he began to hear the real message of God's love and plan of salvation. After a few weeks, Tony accepted Jesus Christ as his Lord and Savior.

"I hope I can stick to this. What happens if I mess up? I mean, I know I can't be good all the time. Things slip out of my mouth that I don't intend to say, and I want a beer sometimes. I get mad at Nick's wife a lot. How can I live the way God wants me to all the time?" Tony asked Rusty.

"You will never be perfect in this life. It is a matter of trusting God to guide and direct your path, and when you slip, you just confess your sin and try to stop doing it. As long as you are sincerely sorry for what you've done, God will forgive you."

Bible Study: Galatians 2

Tony's story gives a modern twist to what Chapter 2 is all about: God's love, acceptance of everyone, setting the right example, and letting go of our old sinful nature to walk by faith. We will never be perfect in this life, but our new integrity will cause us to want to live a victorious Christian life.

We can have the form of godliness—look good and think we're good Christians—but if we're not living by faith and seeking God's guidance, we're only fooling ourselves. If we believe Christ was crucified, then we must also believe that we were crucified with Him, meaning we must be dead to our old nature. When Christ rules our hearts and minds, we are motivated by love and want to be obedient to God (James 1:21–27).

GALATIANS 2:1–10

Fourteen years after his first visit, Paul returned to Galatia and took Barnabas and Titus with him. Paul felt God leading him to visit the church in Galatia again to privately confront the church leaders about their racial partiality of preaching only to the Jews and teaching that strict adherence to the Jewish laws was mandatory. Paul did not want the meeting to become a controversial public issue, lessening the impact of the church on the community and threatening his authority to preach.

Titus, a Greek, could have been circumcised and remained a Christian while adhering to the Jewish laws, but doing so would make it appear circumcision was necessary for his salvation. For this reason he was not circumcised. The Bible teaches that even though something may be legal, if the action detracts from the truth of the gospel, it should be avoided (Rom. 14:21; 1 Cor. 8:13).

> *Even though something may be legal, if it detracts from the truth of the gospel, it should be avoided.*

Some churches impose rules upon their congregants, telling them things such as "Drinking is a sin." While alcohol may be a good thing to avoid, it is not necessarily a sin. Good intentions of church leaders to keep people from doing wrong are positive, but when they place rules on avoiding bad (in their opinion) conduct, they are adding to or taking away from the Word of God. This is also a sin.

Now the Spirit expressly says that in latter times some will depart from the faith, giving heed to deceiving spirits and doctrines of demons, speaking lies in hypocrisy, having their own conscience seared with a hot iron, forbidding to marry, and commanding to abstain from foods which God created to be received with thanksgiving by those who believe and know the truth. For every creature of God is good, and nothing is to be refused if it is received with thanksgiving; for it is sanctified by the word of God and prayer. (1 Tim. 4:1–5)

Paul met with Peter, James, and John and boldly stated that salvation through faith in Jesus Christ is the same for everyone, Jew and gentile alike, even though many in the church thought salvation was intended only for Jews. Some false believers had slipped in to try to deter Paul's message. They were unbending in their belief that Jews must be circumcised and observe their ceremonies and special days while living under the law of Moses.

Paul wasn't intimidated by their position as leaders in the church. He wanted to be sure they understood God had commissioned him to preach the gospel to non-Jews also. He wanted them to know salvation is by faith in Jesus Christ alone, not by adhering to all their laws.

After hearing his case in private, they agreed God had indeed called Paul to preach to the gentiles, and they would continue preaching to the Jews. They only requested Paul help the poor, which he wanted to do anyway.

GALATIANS 2:11–14

Later, in front of all the leaders, Paul confronted Peter for being a hypocrite because he regularly ate with the non-Jews when the Jewish leaders weren't around. But when that conservative group came back from Jerusalem, Peter acted like he had nothing to do with his non-Jewish friends. Peter was fearful of the old traditional Jewish leaders who believed in the Jewish customs, religious ceremonies and holidays, and strict adherence to the law of Moses. Because of Peter, many others in the church had joined in that hypocrisy. Even Barnabas got caught up in the charade.

> *Our walk must match our talk, no matter where we are or who is around to hear us.*

Paul advised Peter that if he acted like a non-Jew when the Jewish leaders weren't watching, he had no right to require non-Jews to conform to Jewish customs just to make a favorable impression on his Jewish leader friends.

GALATIANS 2:15–19

While meeting with the religious leaders in Galatia, Paul told them that Jews had no advantage over non-Jews. No one is made right through righteous living according to the law. Salvation through faith in Jesus Christ alone is available to everyone, not just a select few.

We know Christ paid for our transgressions even though He knew we would periodically fail. Does that mean we are free to live sinful lives, doing whatever we please? Absolutely not! We will fail at times because our sinful nature is not entirely dead, and even if we are trying to be 100 percent devoted to God, our spirit may not agree with our flesh. For instance, "Thou shalt not kill" is a command. While we may not actually kill anyone, we may wish them dead. By even thinking that way, we have murdered in our hearts. Genuine Christian minds are transformed through faith in Jesus Christ.

Salvation is not by works, sacrifices, or ceremonies. It only comes by the grace of God through the sacrifice Jesus Christ made on the cross. While faith has saved us, we are not perfect. If we act like we are faultless, we will be going through the motions, but our hearts will still be sinful by nature.

Paul states that he tried to be the perfect religious leader but was unable to keep at it all the time (Rom. 7:15–20). Once we accept Jesus Christ as our Savior, the new nature God gives us causes us to want to obey all of God's laws, in spirit and in action.

By adding the law to their newfound faith, the Jews got into trouble, because no man can live a perfect life on his own (which is what it would take to obey the whole law). We are dependent upon the grace of God. We are transformed by the renewing of our minds through faith in Jesus Christ. This means we turn from our old ways and walk by faith, trusting in God's guidance for our lives (Rom. 6:1–4).

A Christian obeys out of love, not through fear of condemnation, because when we fall, we know we have forgiveness.

GALATIANS 2:20–21

Before his conversion, Paul's ego had gotten the best of him. It wasn't until he was saved by faith (crucified with Christ) that he was able to live a victorious Christian life. Christ's life was the example Paul now followed. He had died to the law and now entirely identified with Christ. His ego no longer mattered, nor was it essential to him to appear righteous or powerful to others. He lived only to serve God. Paul's life was centered on Christ, who loved him and gave His life for him. Paul's biggest desire was to live in a Christlike manner to show how great God is.

> *Paul's ego no longer mattered, nor was it essential to him that he appear righteous or powerful to others.*

Going back to his former life would have meant abandoning everything Jesus had done for him. Paul refused to go back to the rules, and he lived in a close, personal relationship with Jesus Christ, who frees us to live a life full of love, joy, and peace. Paul did not abuse the grace of God, nor did he serve for the sake of vanity.

Paul stated that if our relationship with God is dependent upon keeping the law, then Christ died for nothing.

Study Questions

GALATIANS 2:1–10

When Paul went to Jerusalem, who did he take with him?

_____

_____

Who did Paul meet while in Jerusalem?

_____

_____

GALATIANS 2:11–14

What was Paul's purpose in meeting with them privately?

_____

_____

Why was it important that Titus was not circumcised?

_____

_____

Paul accepted the Jewish converts as brethren, so why was it so important that he and Barnabas preach to the gentiles? (1 Cor. 1:10)

_____

_____

Should we judge who to reach out to—maybe a homeless person, someone in jail, or others who may be less "socially acceptable"? (Jude 1:19; Gal. 3:28)

_____

_____

GALATIANS 2:15–19

Paul asked them, "Why return to the law if we have been justified by faith?"

_____

_____

Does that mean it isn't necessary to obey all the laws?

_____

_____

Does that allow us to live a careless, sinful life? (Rom. 6:1–4)

_____

_____

GALATIANS 2:20–21

What does Romans 6:6–7 have to say about our sinful nature?

_____

_____

Does that mean we should never sin? (Rom. 7:14–25)

_____

Is self-discipline enough to live a Christian life?

What is false faith? (James 1:21–27)

Personal Application

Do you ever catch yourself thinking you are better than others or that others aren't worth investing your time or talent on? (1 Cor. 2:1–3; 4:6–7; 13:4)

_____

_____

Do you ask God to reveal your shortcomings to you? (Ps. 28:5)

_____

_____

Do you consciously choose to serve God because you love Him, or are you just obeying the rules so you will be saved (false faith)?

_____

_____

Do you ever feel God will grow tired of forgiving you? (Matt. 18:21–22; Rom. 8:1; Acts 3:19)

_____

_____

Something to Ponder

Am I seeking God's direction for my life daily, making
Him my first priority and trusting Him completely?

PRAYER

Thank You, Lord, for loving me in spite of myself, for forgiving me of
my sins and guiding me daily. I pray You will prod my conscience when
I start to drift away and keep me focused on Your everlasting presence in
my life.

Reflections

Use the space provided below to record your reflections on the lesson just completed. Think about the study and all the questions—including the personal application—and record anything that stood out, provided enlightenment, reduced your fears, or enriched your relationship with God.

CHAPTER 3

Holding On:

Fickle vs. Faithful

Now the purpose of the commandment is love from a pure heart, from a
good conscience, and from sincere faith, from which some,
having strayed, have turned aside to idle talk.
1 Timothy 1:5–6

Mike's Story

Sitting in a pew, Mike was thinking. *Well, I went forward and accepted Christ as my Savior. I sure hope the pastor is right that God will forgive me for all I've done. I don't know how I can be saved since I've messed up so much, but I'll take it if it is for real. I'll try to do right.*

I want to learn more about this to be sure I'm saved. I don't want to mess up anymore. I'm going to start reading the Bible to learn more about this.

After church the next week, Brian, a church leader, said, "Hey, Mike, we have a Bible study at my house on Thursday nights. Just a few of us guys get together to talk about and understand the Bible. We have some snacks and chew the fat. It's fun getting to know the other guys better and encourage each other. We need to support and pray for each other. Wanna come?"

"Yeah, that'd be great! I need to get a better handle on this. See you Thursday."

Mike had told his buddy Todd about becoming a Christian. At work the next day, he was excited to tell Todd about the Bible study. "It's gonna be great to meet a bunch of Christian guys and figure out how all this works. I don't understand why, if God didn't save His Son, Jesus, from the cross, how can He forgive me for all I've done?"

"I don't know, man. It all sounds kinda hokey to me. Wanna grab a beer after work? I hear that Trudy gal is pretty hot down at Mac's place."

"Not tonight. I've got to get my car fixed." *I don't want him to think I'm no fun anymore, but I need to stop drinking so much.*

A few days later Todd yelled to Mike across the parking lot as he was heading to his car. "Hey, Mike, we're going to the tavern. Wanna come?"

"No thanks. Still workin' on the car."

"When are you gonna get that thing done? We haven't done much in the last few months. What, do you think you'll go to hell if you have a beer?"

"No, it's just that I need to stop drinking so much. I'm trying to be a better person and live more like God wants me to."

"Boy, that's too bad. You can't have fun anymore. Why not enjoy life? You're never gonna be perfect, so you might as well have fun if you're going to hell anyway. I'm going to hell 'cause that's where all my friends will be, and we're gonna par-tee. Can you honestly say you're happy, Mike?"

"Well, I thought I was having fun when I was running around and drunk all the time, but I never felt comfortable or secure. I always knew something was missing. I just thought I hadn't met the right gal. But for the first time in my life, I am happy, and not because I'm drinking with my friends. I'm just happy within myself. I have peace that I've never felt before."

"Don't you ever miss all those girls we used to party with?"

"Of course I'm tempted at times. I see a good-looking gal and my imagination goes into orbit. But that kind of sex doesn't satisfy. I want a gal who loves me for the person I am, not for the momentary thrill of it all. I want someone in my life who actually cares about me as a person, not how well I perform in the sack."

"Well, if you're tempted, you're going to hell anyway. If you still want booze and fantasize about girls, you're still sinning, from what I understand. So why not enjoy it?"

"That's not true. Jesus was tempted, but He never sinned. Do you think He went to hell? Just because I think about it occasionally doesn't mean I have to do it, and it's not the main thing on my mind anymore. I try to focus on serving God, and I ask Him to help me stop thinking about it."

During one of their get-togethers at Brian's, Mike told Brian about the conversation with Todd. "Do you think I'll go to hell because sometimes I do want to go to the bar and pick up someone?"

"No, that's our natural tendency. God works on us a little at a time—He peels our sins away one layer at a time. Just because you're saved doesn't mean you're perfect. None of us will ever be perfect in this lifetime. God loves us just the way we are, but He'll keep working on us until He calls us home. It's kind of like when you were a child. Your parents got mad at you and may have even punished you, but all along you knew they loved you. They didn't give up on you. That's the way God is, except He's more patient and His love is much greater!"

"How about when I keep making the same mistakes? My mouth goes off quite often. I try hard to stop cussing, but it just comes out when I get mad."

"God knows our weaknesses. He understands our natural tendencies, but little by little He will work on our sins, and eventually we will overcome them if we don't give in. Just ask God to help you become stronger in that area, and He will!"

"So I am saved regardless of my thoughts or deeds as long as I try to live right, and when I slip, I just ask for forgiveness and do my best to stop doing it?"

"That's right. As long as you are sincere when you repent and ask for forgiveness and try to stop sinning, God will forgive you. Just remember, God will not be mocked. So if you're not sincere, don't bother confessing your sins and asking forgiveness. God is not a mean God just waiting for you to mess up. He is a loving heavenly Father who wants to see you succeed. But you cannot con God."

Mike went home and thought about the conversation with Brian. He prayed, *Thank You, Lord, for my salvation. Please show me the areas of my life that I need to change, and help me to make those changes to glorify You.*

Bible Study: Galatians 3

Mike's story is a depiction of the message contained in Chapter 3: God's undying love for us all, His acceptance of us just the way we are, and the forgiveness He offers if we truly repent.

While Satan tries to make us feel we are failing and convince us that God will not continue to forgive, Chapter 3 reveals the truth that God understands our weaknesses, is patient and loving, and will help us overcome our battles with sin and obtain victory over them. God will always forgive if we sincerely try to turn from our sins and glorify Him.

GALATIANS 3:1–5

Paul reminded the Galatians that they had heard of the terrible torment Jesus suffered in His death on the cross, which Jesus chose to endure as a sin offering to cover their (and our) sins. The gift of salvation provided redemption for their sins without the necessity of living under the curse of the law. Paul also reminded the gentiles that they had witnessed many miracles and healings Jesus had performed. They were well aware of Jesus's love for them, His power, and His saving grace.

When the Galatians were with Paul, they accepted the gift of salvation through faith in Jesus Christ. They banded together as believers, just as people often do for a cause for a short time, but their faith was shallow. They had even bonded individually as Christians and groups—with each other and with Jesus—by participating in communion. Here, Paul asks them how they can now be so foolish as to reject salvation through faith and subject themselves to such a critically harsh way of trying to live under the law.

When the rabbis and other leaders began telling them they must follow the laws, the Galatians' faith faltered. The gift of salvation now seemed too good to be true. These religious men were scholars, so the people felt they must have known what they were talking about. The Galatians then began doubting their faith and freedom and started trying to live under the law.

Paul then asked, "How foolish can you be? You've seen all that Christ has done for you. You accepted the gift of salvation through Christ and were no longer subject to the law. Now the rabbis are telling you something different, and you doubt your salvation, which was a gift. Why would you fall for that? Those rules were made by the religious leaders to enslave you to the laws.

"Why would you choose to listen to mere men with their wild ideas? These religious leaders who say you must live under the law are blind to the truth. The only way to ensure your salvation is through faith in Jesus Christ alone. Living by works will serve to condemn rather than save you."

> *The only way to assure your salvation is through faith in Jesus Christ alone.*

Salvation by faith in Jesus Christ really is that easy!

Satan intimidates us by triggering a question in our minds as to God's goodness or our salvation. Often doubts pop into our minds, such as, *If God loved me, He wouldn't allow these things to happen in my life.* If you are battling a particular sin repeatedly, Satan may suggest that you are a fool and a hypocrite, because if you were a "real Christian," you would not continually succumb to that specific sin. If you have a particular weakness or desire, Satan will use it to tempt you, and then he will say something like, "You can't be a real Christian and still desire these things."

Even though our repentance is sincere, we are weak, and death to sin is imperfect in this life. By grace we are saved, but some sins still indwell us, and it is possible for us to fall again and again into the same sin. Until we have utterly defeated a particular sin, it will keep resurfacing. While sin may exasperate us, it cannot have dominion over us once we are saved. What we must remember is to stay on guard, because once we

> *While sin may exasperate us, once we are saved, sin loses its power over us.*

overcome one sin or weakness, Satan will hit us with another. When all is calm and going well, stay on guard—a storm is coming!

GALATIANS 3:6–14

Paul provides an example of God's grace through faith, using Abraham as an example of a faithful, righteous man.

Abraham's salvation was firmly established through the Word and promise of God. There was not a doubt in Abraham's mind. When God told Abraham to take his only son Isaac up to the mountain and sacrifice him on the altar, he did so without question.

Abraham realized God's command was a test of his faith. Even though he was filled with anxiety, Abraham knew God would not take his son because He had already promised that He would provide many descendants through Isaac (Gen. 12:7). Because Abraham obeyed, God accepted him as a righteous man and blessed him by saving his son Isaac (Gen. 22:1–13).

God's curse is against all sinners. Those who live by the law are cursed because all fall short of the law's standards. It is arrogant to think we can live by the law successfully. It is only through faith that we become righteous. Justification by faith is not a new doctrine, for it was taught in the synagogue—which was the Old Testament church of God—long before the gospel was preached.

The only way we can be delivered from the curse of the law and regain God's grace is through faith in Christ. Christ redeemed us from that curse by becoming a sin offering for us. He was made a curse for us. In other words, while He was never separated from God, He took the consequences of our sinful choices and suffered extreme punishment to atone for our sins. Christians living by faith are spiritual sons and daughters of Abraham, regardless of their ethnicity or gender.

What many fail to appreciate fully is the terrible torment and sacrifice Jesus went through so He could offer us the blessings of Abraham. It was Jesus's choice to endure unbearable pain and suffering, giving His mortal life as a sacrifice for our sins because He loves us. Many accept this without due consideration because it is more than we can imagine or understand. Our failure to comprehend the measure of His sacrifice is a dreadful mistake, and a costly one if we fail to accept salvation by faith in Jesus Christ alone.

The horrible suffering and torment Jesus endured should be a loud warning to sinners to repent and turn from their wicked ways. If mankind doesn't repent and accept Christ as their personal Savior through faith, their punishment will be greater than the curses of the law.

Galatians 3:15–18

If God did not spare Christ from the cross, how can He so freely forgive our sins? Christ invites sinners to take refuge in Him through faith. Because of His sacrifice on the cross, we can be assured of our salvation. The promises were first made to Christ, and through Him, passed on to those who, by faith, become one with Christ in spirit. Our changed lives and nature cause us to want to live by moral laws out of love for God through our faith. Proof of our faith is evident through our changed lives.

Does that mean we must live by the rules or perish? No! When the promise is mingled with the law, it becomes nothing but the law. Those who live by the law are cursed, because all fall short of the standards of the law. If we cling to justification by works under the law, as the Galatians were doing, we are rejecting God's gift of grace. But after accepting Christ as our Savior, we must keep our eyes on Him. This focus will cause us to want to live in a Christlike manner.

Occasionally we will fail because our evil nature still exists to some degree, but our focus will be on God. Anyone who thinks his salvation depends solely on living a sin-free life because he has been saved is fooling himself and is prideful to think he can master such a feat. When we slip (which we all will), we must turn from our sins, repent, and ask forgiveness. God is faithful to forgive a righteous man (Rom. 3:23–31).

GALATIANS 3:19–22

The law was first given by God's ministry of angels to Moses, the mediator between God and the Jewish people. The purpose was to cause men to see their sinfulness and to point to Christ, through whom they could be pardoned and justified.

If we are free to live as we choose, why was the law even necessary? Because before Christ died for our sins, there was a need to reform the depraved lives people were living and to point people to the coming Messiah. The laws were established to bring the sinful lives of the Israelites back to a standard of morality. When we accept Jesus Christ as our Savior, we no longer need the law and will choose to live righteously before God, thereby erasing the need for the law. The law then would serve only to put us under bondage and lessen our faith in God.

GALATIANS 3:23–25

The law did not teach knowledge that would save, but by the law and its sacrifices, it pointed to Christ. It leads to the way of justification and salvation, which is only by faith in Christ.

Most people choose to go about their daily lives living as they want. Either they don't believe in God or they make light of the gospel. Many have other, self-serving gods. Lulled by Satan, they revel in worldly pleasures, interests, and pursuits.

Some say they believe and are saved, but they only go through the motions of attending a church, with no other evidence of their salvation. Some go through the motions of putting on a good front, but behind closed doors is another story. Some use prayer times within the church to look pious and gossip about others, not realizing they are sinning. There are many ways in which people fool themselves. Without Christ, we are easily fooled into sinful living. But the awakened sinner discovers his dreadful condition and realizes the grace of God is his only real hope.

Paul then asks, "Why would you choose to listen to mere men and their wild ideas?" These religious leaders who say you must live under the law have been blinded so they can't see they can trust in Christ crucified. The only way to ensure your salvation is through faith in Jesus Christ alone—works will not save you and the law won't save you. But through the Holy Spirit, it becomes a duty you love and your standard for daily self-examination.

Without Christ, the sinner is judged on his merit. Talk is cheap, but a Christian life will reflect God's love and goodness to all. A Christian learns to depend on the Savior and find rest in the fact that he is no longer condemned, but is instead saved by grace (Rom. 8:1).

GALATIANS 3:26–29

Salvation is available to all ethnicities and genders who receive Jesus Christ as their Lord and Savior through faith and belief.

The changes that take place in a Christian's heart by relying on Christ alone for justification and salvation are significant and evident in their lives. We become new people and do our best to live sin-free lives for the glory of God. We do not secure salvation through proclamation or works. We now seek God's direction for our lives. As Christians, we love Him with all our hearts, souls, and minds, and trust Him completely to guide our way. We also learn to love others as ourselves, meaning we endeavor to meet the needs of others even when it's inconvenient. Serving God is now our priority.

Baptism does not save us; it serves to identify us with Christ. It is symbolic of the burial of our old life (going under the water), and coming up out of the water symbolizes our resurrection into a new life. We are declaring that we are no longer slaves to our sinful lives, but in newness of life, are capable of hearing from and responding to God.

The difference between a sinner and a Christian is this: The sinner lives by the law to stay out of trouble and impress others by looking saintly in their eyes. The Christian, on the other hand, seeks God's direction and will abide by the laws because of his now loving, Christlike nature. He learns to depend upon the Savior and lives only to glorify God.

Study Questions

When Paul preached the gospel of Christ, how did the Galatians respond?

_____

_____

Did they partake of communion?

_____

_____

Why were they so easily swayed?

_____

_____

What example did Paul use to prove God's grace?

_____

_____

What did Abraham do that proved his faith in God? (Gen. 22:1–13)

_____

_____

Why was Abraham so sure God would bless him? (Gen. 12:7)

_____

_____

Against whom is God's curse?

_____

_____

What was the purpose of the law?

_____

_____

What is the only way to salvation?

_____

_____

If God didn't spare His Son from the cross, how can He forgive us?

_____

_____

To whom is salvation available? (John 3:16; Eph. 2:8–9)

_____

_____

What happens if we mingle the promise of God with the law?

_____

Who was the law administered by, and to whom?

_____

_____

To whom was the promise of salvation given?

_____

_____

Is it possible for God's law to be contrary to the gospel of Christ?

_____

_____

Do most people trust in God's promises and follow Christ? Why or why not?

_____

_____

What is the difference of the law between sinners and Christians?

_____

_____

By accepting Christ, how will we change?

_____

_____

What are some of the ways Satan tries to deceive believers?

_____

_____

How can we combat those deceptions?

_____

_____

Personal Application

Have you ever questioned your salvation because you felt you weren't good enough?

_____

_____

If so, would that make you more susceptible to false doctrines?

_____

_____

If a particular sin keeps resurfacing in your life, do you believe you are still saved?

_____

_____

Have you noticed any changes in yourself since receiving Christ as your Savior?

_____

_____

_____

What has changed?

_____

_____

_____

Are you living a godly life so others will think you are a Christian, or are you seeking God's direction for your life and listening when He informs you of your weaknesses?

_____

_____

Something to Ponder

Do I live a godly life so others will know I am a Christian
or because I seek God's direction for my life and
listen when He reveals my weaknesses to me?

PRAYER

Thank You, Lord, for loving me in spite of myself, for always forgiving me and showing me the things I need to change. You are with me at all times, leading and guiding my path. I pray You will reveal any areas of contention that I may not be aware of, and help me to turn from any wicked ways within.

Reflections

Use the space provided below to record your reflections on the lesson just completed. Think about the study and all the questions—including the personal application—and record anything that stood out, provided enlightenment, reduced your fears, or enriched your relationship with God.

CHAPTER 4

The Difference between Legalism and Justification through Faith

For by grace you have been saved by faith, and that not of yourselves;
it is the gift of God, not of works, lest anyone should boast.
Ephesians 2:8–9

Stacy's Story

Sitting down at the table after a hard day at the office, Stacy thought, *I've got to hurry and get this Bible study done before everyone gets here tomorrow. I've been so busy with choir practice and going to church services and committee meetings that I haven't had time to get this lesson done. I sure hope God appreciates all I'm doing for Him.*

"Mommy, can we go to the park? I want to go play with the other kids. Please?"

"I'm sorry, honey. I'm just too busy. Maybe Saturday."

"Please, Mommy? I haven't got to go in a long time."

"I'm sorry, honey. It's just been really busy at work and at church. Go play with Judy next door."

Slumping over the table, Stacy thought, *It would be nice to spend more time with her, but I've got to do the Lord's work. I can't let everyone down; they'll think I don't care enough to get involved.*

Later that evening, her husband, Josh, called out, "Hon, come watch this movie with me."

"In a bit. I've got to finish this study."

A while later she joined Josh to watch the movie he had selected. It was a bit racy, so when some seductive scenes came on, she jumped up and said, "No, we can't watch that. I don't think God would approve."

"They didn't say any nasty words. Come on, let's watch it."

"No. If you want to watch it, go ahead, but I'm going to do what our Lord wants me to do."

"Okay, we'll watch the news. I just wish once in a while we could watch a movie without you getting so upset."

The news came on, and as usual, it was all negative. Then the newscaster started bashing a politician, and his language included some crude words.

"Turn it off," said Stacy. "I'm sick and tired of always having to hear people cursing and using God's name in vain."

"Oh, you're such a prude. Can't we watch anything without you getting upset?"

"I need to guard my thoughts so I don't offend the Lord."

"Whatever. Go do what you have to do for the church. I'm going to watch the movie."

"Okay, fine!"

Getting back into her Bible study, Stacy was upset that she and Josh had been having so much trouble lately. *I wish I could watch something with him or go do something fun, but I know I'm supposed to be doing God's work, and I can't get sidetracked by all this worldly stuff.*

Her best friend, Trudy, called and said, "Hey, we're having a party Saturday. We're going to have a mariachi band here, margaritas, and a deejay. Everyone from the block will be here. It's going to be a blast. Can you and Josh make it?"

"I'm sorry, but that's not what my Lord would want me to do. I am supposed to be spreading the gospel and working for Him. I don't have time to go to parties, and I don't think God wants us to be drinking and partying all the time."

"Can't you do anything for fun anymore? You've kind of shut me out the past few months."

I wish I could have more fun, but my Lord comes first. He wouldn't want me to do all this stuff. He wants me working for His cause. Dad would never have gone to parties or watched movies like Josh wanted me to watch. Dad preached the Word and told us we should live sober lives dedicated to the Lord. Since I've come back to God, I need to abide by the rules.

While shopping for groceries, Stacy ran into Trudy. "Hi, Stacy. Sure wish you could make it to the party. It's going to be a blast! Please come, Stacy. It's going to be fun!"

"I can't do that kind of stuff anymore. I'm supposed to be dedicated to the Lord now."

"Ever hear the term 'So heavenly minded, you're no earthly good'? God never intended for us to live like hermits, working so hard we forget to live. He said to live life joyously! For instance, God didn't say we couldn't drink; He said not to drink excessively. If you stay inside your house studying the Bible and praying all day and don't get involved in anything or anyone other than church people, how are you ever going to reach the lost?"

"Good point. I'll have to think about that," Stacy replied.

"I hope you do. I miss talking to you and doing things."

On the way home, Stacy thought about her conversation with Trudy. *Well, God did turn water into wine. Maybe it's okay to drink a little, and she's right about mixing with people outside the church too. How will I ever spread the gospel to unbelievers if I don't talk to them? I guess we could go to the party.*

Bible Study: Galatians 4

This story provides a modern-day twist to what Chapter 4 is all about: salvation by grace through believing in and trusting God for our salvation, not by our own efforts. We don't need to work out our salvation, nor do we need to stop enjoying life. We just need to seek God's guidance, trusting Him to show us what we should or shouldn't be doing (Prov. 16:8; Ps. 37:23). He said we should have a joyous life (John 10:10). If we trust God to guide our paths, we can live even more joyously than before we were saved, because we know we have a loving heavenly Father who will guide and direct our paths. We can trust that He will prod our conscience if we start to drift away and will gently pull us back to Himself.

We don't need to work to prove ourselves. We just need to trust God for our salvation, obey His promptings, and enjoy life!

GALATIANS 4:1–7

The original covenant with Abraham did not contain a list of laws. The laws were added later to shed light on the right and wrong behaviors of the Jewish people and to restrain their misconduct. The rules were added to show them the errors of their ways and teach them how they should live.

Just as a child has a tendency to be self-centered and mischievous before a parent teaches them how they should act, the Jewish people were beginning to live self-serving, prideful, greedy, lustful, lawless lives. They had no higher compass to direct them.

The laws Moses presented were established to bring a sense of order to their lives and prepare the way for Christ's arrival. The Jewish people did not entirely understand the meaning of the laws, and so the Jewish leaders started adding to the requirements, putting people under bondage to their rites and observances. Laws allow us to focus on behaviors by which we can measure our performance. By observing the law, we feel a sense of achievement, but when we hang on to this as our basis for salvation, we are taking the focus off Christ and putting it back on ourselves. The natural tendency of the Jewish people was still self-serving. They obeyed the law mostly in fear of retaliation. Their natural tendencies were still selfish. They did not grasp the concept and revelation of Christ's sacrifice for their sins.

Once a child becomes old enough to understand how life works and what is right and wrong, they no longer need a parent telling them every move to make. Once the Jews were able to understand and accept God's grace, His death on the cross, and the great sacrifice He made to cover their sins, they were no longer subject to the old laws.

While some Galatians received the message of Christ, many refused to listen and continued under bondage so they would appear righteous to others in their community. The few who believed that Jesus Christ was their Savior were adopted into the family of God and were no longer slaves to the Jewish laws.

The Holy Spirit enables believers to recognize this truth and witness to others about their new relationship with God, causing them to turn from their wicked ways because of their thankfulness and love for Him.

Evidence of true believers is through their changed lives. They now want to serve God because they recognize His great sacrifice, and with thankful, reverent hearts and love for God, they want to work for Him. Their natural tendency now is to love others as Christ first loved them.

GALATIANS 4:8–11

Paul reminds the Christians that they used to be under bondage to the law or worship false gods, but they were freed from that bondage when they accepted Christ's gift of salvation.

He asks, "Why are you turning back to the laws now? Whatever you love the most has a tendency to be your god. Why can't you accept the simplicity of the gospel of Christ? Christ died for your sins. You think you are serving God by being under bondage to the laws? If so, you are sorely mistaken. God did not put all those restrictions and requirements on you—the Jewish leaders added those."

> *Whatever you value and love the most is your god!*

God loved you and knew you before you knew Him. He accepted you as His heir when you received the message and believed that Jesus died for your sins. Why do you try to complicate it? It is that simple! The more mercy you receive, the more you want to serve God.

We Christians should learn to examine our own lives and not be content that we are pretty good. We need to ask God to reveal our sins and then help us turn from our wicked ways, not just because the law says we have to, but because God reveals our sins to us when we ask Him to guide us.

Paul asks the Galatians, "Did I labor in vain? Didn't you get the message? The grace of God saves you. God directs your new nature, not the law. How can you turn back and be enslaved to the law again when you were free through God's grace? That is what you are doing when you think you have to work so hard at obeying the law."

Paul does not hint that the Galatians have lost their salvation, but he wants them to question themselves to see if they ever really believed they were saved through Christ's sacrifice.

We must remember to make God the priority in our lives and seek His direction, and we will not fail because He will direct our paths.

GALATIANS 4:12–18

Paul reminds them of how they welcomed him when he first came to them. They had established a close bond, and the Galatians had even cared for him when he was ill. He didn't understand why they now turned on him, treating him almost as an enemy.

They may have thought of Paul as their enemy, but he assured them he was their friend. He felt as though they were his children because he had first ministered the gospel of Christ to them and had established such a close bond with them.

The Galatians had turned back to the law and were allowing the Jewish leaders to add to it and place them under bondage to the ceremonies and rituals. Paul is asking them to follow his example once again and abandon the ceremonial rites and restrictions of Judaism. Instead, he wants them to seek God's direction and counsel.

The religious leaders of the church had drawn the Galatians away from the truth of the gospel because they wanted control of the church. The mark of a false teacher is that they are not focused on leading people to Christ, but they use people to build up themselves and their works. We need to beware of those who demand exclusive allegiance to their particular ministries because they say they are the only ones who are right. The Jewish religious leaders pretended to care about the Galatians, but were not sincere or upright; they just wanted positions of power.

Paul tells the Galatians that it is good to be passionate about their salvation, but that passion can be misguided. They cannot be on fire for God one minute, then worried they are not abiding by the laws the next. They need to be consistent in their faith. They would lead much happier lives if they weren't under the bondage of the law, but recognized that their freedom comes through the grace of God.

Galatians 4:19–20

Paul wasn't sure where the Galatians stood as far as recognizing that salvation was only by the grace of God. The proof of their salvation lay in the fact that they trusted in God alone for their salvation. Their changed lives would be evidence of the Holy Spirit living within them, and they would no longer live to please themselves, but to love others and expose the darkness surrounding them.

Galatians 4:21–27

Paul draws an analogy of the difference between living under the law and living freely through the grace of God.

Since Sarah was unable to conceive, she told Abraham to go to Hagar that she might be able to provide him with an heir. Sarah did not believe she would ever be able to have a child. Hagar, as a bond servant, had to perform as her owner instructed, and this resulted in an illegitimate son, Ishmael.

The Jewish people who lived under the law were similar in that they were obeying the rules, but there was no real love there—no real connection to God. They were under the bondage of the laws.

But God had promised Abraham he would have a son with Sarah. She finally conceived and brought forth Isaac, Abraham's beloved son. When Isaac was born, he was very much loved because he was a child of promise.

The Galatians who accepted the gift of salvation were adopted into the family of God, and there is a real connection there—they are family! A son obeys his father out of love, while a servant obeys out of fear. We are the sons and daughters of God. God promises salvation to anyone who accepts and professes Jesus Christ as their Lord and Savior.

Galatians 4:28–31

Ishmael continually persecuted Isaac because he knew Isaac would inherit everything Abraham had. Ishmael had no claim to any of it since he had been born under bondage.

Hagar (his mother) was a bond servant who was ordered to conceive and provide Abraham and Sarah with a child. Hagar obliged, not because she wanted to, but because it was her duty. She and Ishmael were eventually sent away.

That is the way many of the Galatians received the laws. They were compelled to follow the rules to stay out of trouble. It was not a conversion of the heart. They were under bondage to the law. These were not true believers, and they did not receive salvation.

> *A son obeys out of love; a servant, out of fear. We are the sons and daughters of God.*

Works done by man's own strength, while they may be legal, may not be right or in their best interests. When men do good things because they believe it is necessary for their salvation and they neglect the promise of God, they act according to the law (Eph. 2:8–9). Living in a manner to obey the law, a person is reentering slavery and is never at rest until he returns to his dependence on Christ. This type of bondage is a spirit of persecution and keeps a man on edge: What should I do next to gain points?

Just like Sarah and Hagar (or Isaac and Ishmael) could not be reconciled, it is impossible for law and grace (the flesh and the spirit) to be reconciled by compromise and stay together.

We who believe in Jesus Christ as Lord and Savior know that we, too, are children of promise. We walk in the light and let God guide and direct our paths.

We rely on the fact that God loves us the way we are but helps us grow closer to Him by gently and lovingly prodding us to go another route.

Let us rest in the goodness of God. Search the Scriptures, meditate on them, pray, and seek God's guidance. That is the way to a Spirit-filled life overflowing with peace and love.

NOTE:

"Legalism" doesn't just mean the setup of spiritual standards. We do have rules set for us, and we live by them out of love. Legalism means worshiping those standards and thinking we are spiritual because we obey them (focusing on us again, and our works). It also often means judging others by these standards instead of letting God be the judge.

We can't change the law or our old nature.

We can't compromise grace by adding just a little bit of law.

What we can do with legalism is cast it out and rely entirely on grace.

Study Questions

GALATIANS 4:1–7

Why were the laws written?

_____

_____

Did all the gentiles accept the message of Christ?

_____

_____

What does the Holy Spirit enable believers to do?

_____

_____

What is the evidence of a true believer?

_____

_____

GALATIANS 4:8–11

How were the Galatians treating Paul?

_____

_____

Why?

_____

Why was Paul so concerned for them?

What does Paul say all Christians should do?

What is Paul asking them to question about themselves?

GALATIANS 4:12–18

Were the Galatians living by faith?

What is Paul asking them to do?

Why did the Jewish leaders add the ceremonies and rituals to the laws?

Why does Paul tell them to watch their passion for serving God?

_____

_____

Why is that important?

_____

_____

GALATIANS 4:19–20

What feelings did Paul have for the Galatians?

_____

_____

What are the criteria for salvation?

_____

_____

GALATIANS 4:21–27

What analogy does Paul use to describe the difference between bondage and salvation through Christ's sacrifice?

_____

_____

If you live under the law, are you really saved?

_____

GALATIANS 4:28–31

Why did the Galatians live so rigorously by the law?

_____

_____

What happens when you believe your salvation depends upon obeying the law?

_____

_____

Why do Christians live the way they ought to? Is it by the law or something else? If so, what?

_____

_____

How does God direct our paths?

_____

_____

How can we draw closer to God?

_____

_____

Personal Application

Do you ever feel you must live by the letter of the law to be saved? (Gal. 5:4; Eph. 2:8–9)

_____

_____

How does God direct your path? (1 Cor. 2:14; 2 Tim. 3:16; Prov. 3:6)

_____

_____

Do you ever feel God is displeased with you because you're not working hard enough? (John 6:28–29; Rom. 4:4)

_____

_____

Do you know beyond a shadow of a doubt that you are saved regardless of what you do for the church? (1 John 2:1–2; Eph. 3:17–21)

_____

_____

_____

Do you really believe it can be as simple as accepting Christ as your Savior and letting Him direct your path? (Rom. 10:8–10; 2 Tim. 1:8–10)

_____

_____

_____

Do I believe God loves me and is with me at all times? Do I know without a doubt that He loves me despite my failures?

_____

_____

Something to Ponder

Am I really confident I am saved regardless of whether or not I abide by all the church rules or work hard enough in the church?

PRAYER

Thank You, Lord, for loving me and forgiving all my sins. Help me to understand the difference between law and grace. Show me the areas of my life that are not pleasing to You, and help me live a righteous, holy life glorifying only You.

Reflections

Use the space provided below to record your reflections on the lesson just completed. Think about the study and all the questions—including the personal application—and record anything that stood out, provided enlightenment, reduced your fears, or enriched your relationship with God.

CHAPTER 5

Love Demonstrates Faith

But when the kindness and the love of God our Savior toward man appeared, not by works of righteousness which we have done, but according to His mercy He saved us, through the washing of regeneration and renewing of the Holy Spirit, whom He poured out on us abundantly through Jesus Christ our Savior, that having been justified by His grace we should become heirs according to the hope of eternal life.

Titus 3:4–7

Cindy's Story

Driving home from church, Cindy remarked to her husband, Dan, "Boy, that was a good sermon today, wasn't it?"

"Yeah. He sure makes you stop and think about where you're headed."

"Do you think we need to worry about every word that comes out of our mouths?"

"Well, a sin is a sin. But I think God knows we're not perfect, and as long as we try to live sinless lives and ask God to help us change, He will forgive our sins."

"Are you sure? I mean, I try to do everything right, but when I get upset my mouth keeps going off again and again. How many times will God forgive me for that?"

"The Bible says He will keep forgiving as long as we are sincere and seek His help in changing those things that are not pleasing to Him," Dan replied.

"What about speaking in tongues? The pastor said we need to speak in tongues or we are not saved."

"That is something you'll need to scour the Word for to find the answers. Sometimes churches make up their own rules, but the Bible is the final authority. Check it out!"

"Good point. I will go online and check out every reference there is and then test those against what the Bible has to say about it."

"Besides, Cindy, what did the Lord say was the greatest commandment and criteria for salvation? He said, 'Love the Lord your God with all your heart, all your soul, and all your mind,' and the second commandment was to love your neighbor as yourself. Don't you think those would cause you to live a life that pleases God?"

"I suppose so," Cindy said. "But why is it so hard to live a godly life?"

"Because we are in a spiritual war. Satan wants us to fear failure, experiences, and people. He tries to place doubts in our minds all the time. What we have to remember is that we have a loving heavenly Father who knows all our doubts and fears and waits for us to call upon Him for His guidance and protection. God is always in control. We need to remember that and rely on Him and ask Him for directions when we are confused or doubting."

Bible Study: Galatians 5

This story is intended to illustrate the message contained in Galatians 5. In this chapter, we find that Satan can use Christians and others to cause us to doubt our salvation by putting specific rules on Christianity.

The best way to know for sure that you are saved is by asking Jesus to be your Lord and Savior. After taking that step, give God the first part of your day by studying the Word and praying.

When any person or organization says something that does not align with what you believe, there are numerous ways to find the truth in God's Word. Go to any search engine online and type in your questions. Then go to your Bible to verify the answers. The online resource will usually give you the verses to back up what it is saying.

When you pray, be sure to focus on God's presence in your life. His Holy Spirit has indwelled you and is always available for soul-searching and counsel. God loves you and is with you to provide your needs. He always forgives a sinner when they have a sincere desire to turn from their wicked ways and serve Him.

GALATIANS 5:1–6

Many Galatians were getting circumcised to observe the Jewish laws. What they failed to realize is that by becoming circumcised, they were implying a commitment to do everything the law said. Paul reminded them that they must rely solely on Christ as their Savior and not succumb to the rules of the Jewish religious leaders. By submitting to circumcision, they were in effect putting themselves back under bondage to the Jewish laws. When you accept a part of the law as necessary for your salvation, you are committing to all of the law and alienating yourself from Christ.

> *If we depend on Jesus plus our good works, we are in effect saying Jesus's life is not worthy enough to cover our sins. At that point, we are cut off from God.*

If we submit to manmade religious laws, rites, or ceremonies to earn our salvation, we turn from grace and forfeit our salvation. It is not that there is anything wrong with the action taken (e.g., circumcision or whatever); it's just wrong if that action is taken with the belief that it will earn salvation or is a requirement to retain salvation. It's a fundamental problem that whenever we make our salvation dependent on Jesus plus anything else, instead of Jesus only, then we are in effect saying that His life was not worthy enough to cover our particular deeds and needs.

At that point we are cut off from God. We are in effect saying Christ is not enough! We have rejected the free gift of salvation through grace and must live a perfect life according to religious laws. For example, we must never sin, and that is an impossible feat for a mere man. Our hope of salvation through Jesus Christ is gone.

It does not matter if we actually try to live a perfect life or if we completely disregard the law. The criterion for our salvation is faith in Christ, as expressed through love for the Lord our God and love for each other.

Accepting Jesus Christ as Lord and Savior is the only criterion for our salvation. Anything else is useless and of no value. Evidence of Christian faith is demonstrated by faith working through love, being thankful for our salvation, loving God first and foremost, and loving others as ourselves. That's it!

> *Faith expressed through accepting Jesus Christ is the only criterion for our salvation.*

GALATIANS 5:7–12

Paul did not understand why some of the Galatians had turned back to the law. He still felt that those who had trusted in the gospel initially would return to again adopt the gospel of Christ.

The religious leaders were not only distorting the truth, but were also spreading lies about Paul. They asserted he had preached circumcision both before and after coming to Christ, when in truth, after his conversion he had only taught the message of the cross. Many of the Galatians believed the lies and persecuted Paul for being a hypocrite.

Paul was discouraged because many of the Galatians had gone back to the law to ensure their salvation. Paul asked them why they would turn back to bondage when they were doing so well in serving God. He then inquired by what means the religious leaders were able to persuade them to go back to servitude under the law. Paul admonished the Galatians that the religious scholars were deluding them. These same scholars were wrong in judging them, and Paul added that their words were most likely driven by Satan himself.

> *Sometimes churches make up their own rules, but the Bible is the final authority. If in doubt, check it out!*

Sometimes Christians will say you need to abide by certain rules or do certain things to ensure your salvation. If someone tells you to do something other than what you know to be true through studying the Word yourself, check it out. We need to be very careful about who we listen to and verify that they are speaking truthfully. God's Word is our final authority. False teaching, left unchecked, permeates and harms the church. Just as one spark can start a forest fire, one misguided person can spread falsehood and discord among church members.

Paul told the Galatians to hold fast to their faith. Salvation is more than lip service; it is evidenced by our changed lives. Many start out as firm believers but are swayed by peer pressure, religious scholars, or circumstances surrounding their lives. They may begin to doubt and turn away from the truth of the gospel.

The Jews were offended because Paul encouraged the Galatians to cut off relations with the legalists. Paul preached Christ as the only way to salvation for sinners. If he had agreed that observance of the law of Moses was to be joined with faith in Christ as necessary for salvation, then those early believers might have avoided many of the sufferings they underwent. But false teaching should be nipped in the bud. Those who persist in subverting the gospel will fall under the judgment of God.

The Jewish religious leaders persuaded the Galatians that the message of the cross wasn't enough to ensure their salvation. They said the Galatians also needed to observe the Jewish rites, customs, and ceremonies. They may have said something like, "If you were a true Christian, you wouldn't do that."

Religious leaders who deem themselves superior—placing rules and restrictions on you as necessary for your salvation—are deluded and wrong in judging you, and their words may be driven by Satan himself. The proof of truth can always be found in the Word of God. Test everything and everyone for evidence of the facts.

GALATIANS 5:13–15

The teachings of Jewish laws are incompatible with the gospel of Christ. Christians are called to enjoy the rights and blessings of freedom from the law. Paul reminds the Galatians that they no longer need to live under the law of Moses, which obligated them to follow rules, restrictions, and other rites and ceremonies. He emphasized they were now free to live godly lives serving God and others.

God's law is love. First, we are to love God, then we are to love others as ourselves. That is all that is required. If we live that way, putting God and others first, our rules of conduct will line up similar to Jewish law as far as moral conduct, but we will live this way out of love rather than fear.

This does not give Christians the right to abuse their newfound freedom. It is not an excuse to indulge in sinfulness. The gospel of Christ compels us to godliness (1 John 3:6-9) and does not give us permission to return to sin. While our old corrupt nature still resides within us, we are no longer under its control. The Holy Spirit empowers us and creates a desire to live godly lives.

It is not enough to tell others that we are Christians. We must reflect Christian behavior, which is only possible if we are being led by the Holy Spirit. When we rely on God to direct our paths, our conduct will automatically reflect Christian values and glorify God.

Paul's efforts to restore the Galatians back to the idea of fundamental Christianity was hindered by the conflicts not only among the Jewish leaders, but also among members of the church and other influences. Pride and envy caused many quarrels among the church members. They were gossiping and judging each other, creating much discord.

Our efforts to please God in our own strength usually result in sinful behaviors. The works of the flesh are of Satan. Actions that characterize the flesh are sexual immorality, unrestrained passion for anything or anyone, spirituality (idolatry, sorcery), using magic in an attempt to manipulate people, demonic beings, gods, or drugs used to induce euphoric religious experiences, hostility, strife, contentiousness that causes division, and social sins such as drunkenness, carousing (being on the prowl for sinful pleasure), immorality, or any deviant sexual activity, including adultery, fornication, bestiality, and homosexuality. This is not an exhaustive list (see Rom. 1:29–31; 1 Cor. 6:9–10).

> *Many who profess Christianity live by works of the flesh and hope for salvation, but without the new nature the Holy Spirit provides, those actions count for nothing.*

Many who profess Christianity live by works of the flesh and hope for salvation, but without the new nature the Holy Spirit provides, those actions count for nothing.

When following sinful desires, Christians begin criticizing and quarreling with others in the church. For instance, in one church I attended, the deacons and elders were bickering among themselves about the color choices for the carpeting in the sanctuary. They were so adamant in their views that they got the whole church involved in the dispute. Isn't that silly? It was a power play. The egos got involved and brought about much discord, causing several members to leave the church. That is nothing more than our sinful nature in action.

By accepting the gospel of Christ, our new spiritual nature compels us to serve others through love, which is the fulfillment of the gospel of Christ. The highest command is to love the Lord your God with all your heart, and love your neighbor as yourself.

> *You shall love the Lord your God with all your heart, with all your soul, with all your strength, and with all your mind, and your neighbor as yourself.*
> Luke 10:27

GALATIANS 5:16–26

As Christians, we can be tempted to view our freedom in Christ as an opportunity to do as we please. Our sinful nature still resides in us, but we are to rely on the Holy Spirit to guide and direct our paths.

Those who allow sinful patterns to rule will not inherit the kingdom of God. We do not obey the law to secure our salvation, but rather because we love and serve the living God, who empowers us to love others as ourselves, leaving our sinful natures (and egos) behind.

We no longer live under the law of Moses. Christ now empowers us through the Holy Spirit to live godly lives, loving and serving one another through our attitudes and actions. This is not an automatic transformation, because our sinful nature is still at odds with the Holy Spirit. We must make a conscious choice to submit to the leadership of the Holy Spirit day by day and moment by moment.

> *We must make a conscious choice to submit to the leadership of the Holy Spirit day by day and moment by moment.*

We need to remember we are in spiritual warfare. Satan will try to tempt or deceive us into submitting to our lower natures, which are at odds with what the Holy Spirit desires for us.

The devil may cause us to envy others who have achieved a certain status or goal while we have not yet attained such a position; we then become jealous. When this happens, we must realize we are not empowering the Holy Spirit to direct our path, and we must cry out to God to help us submit to His leading. It is essential to keep our focus on God and seek His direction. Otherwise, we will succumb to the desires of the flesh.

When the Holy Spirit is empowering us, many gifts—such as affection for others, exuberance about life, serenity, and confidence—become evident in our lives. We no longer flit from one belief of salvation and grace to another. We are confident about our salvation, and we are compassionate, genuinely caring about the needs of others.

We tend to see the good in others, recognizing that God instilled basic goodness in all people. We are loyal to our commitments and able to marshal and direct our energies wisely.

When living under the law, those tendencies are nowhere to be found. We feel deprived, so we drift off and do whatever makes us feel good as long as we're not breaking the law. Our sinful nature harbors jealousy, pride, arrogance, greed, lust, and myriad tendencies of the flesh.

When led by the Holy Spirit, we do not just hold it as an idea in our heads or a sentiment in our hearts, but we work out its implications in every detail of our lives. This means we will not compare ourselves with another, as if one is better than the other. We have far more worthy things to do with our lives. Each of us is an original design of God's making, and He has a purpose for each of our lives.

Guarding ourselves so we won't sin is not enough. We need to set the example for others to follow. We need to be there for one another, showering each other with God's love. We also need to guard our conversations, because we will be held accountable for them. That means no off-color remarks and no gossiping or hurtful discussions. We are to build each other up and help equip other saints to spread the gospel.

Our new nature will cause us to consciously turn from any unhealthy, sinful thoughts, conversations, or deeds and walk in the newness of life. We are not to desire esteem or power, nor are we to provoke or envy others. Our job is to bring out the best in ourselves and others, all to the glory of God.

Study Questions

GALATIANS 5:1–6

Must we obey all the rules set forth by the church? (Titus 3:5; Eph. 2:8–9)

_____

_____

If we are true Christians, what happens if we sin? (1 John 1:9)

_____

_____

What are the criteria for being saved? (John 3:16; Matt. 22:36–40)

_____

_____

How do we demonstrate Christianity to the world? (Gal. 5:22)

_____

_____

GALATIANS 5:7–12

Should we believe everything a religious leader or other Christian tells us? (1 Thess. 5:19–22)

_____

_____

How can we be sure we know the truth?

_____

_____

GALATIANS 5:13–15

What is the greatest and only valid law of God? (Matt. 22:36–40)

_____

_____

Since we are Christians, are we free to sin?

_____

_____

GALATIANS 5:16–26

Why is it so hard to live a godly life all the time? (Eph. 6:12)

_____

_____

How can we live a victorious Christian life? (Eph. 6:10–20)

_____

Is it okay to profess Christianity but only get serious about it as a weekend warrior? (2 Cor. 5:17; Matt. 7:21–23)

_____

_____

If we continue to allow our sinful nature to dominate our lives (even though we profess Christianity), are we still saved?

_____

_____

Personal Application

Do I know for sure that I am saved?

_____

_____

When a Christian tells me I am not living as I should, do I check it out in the Word?

_____

_____

Do I let my ego, conversations, greed, or lusts overrule my desire to serve God?

_____

_____

Am I putting God first in my life? Is He my priority?

_____

Do I spend time with Him every day?

_____

_____

Do I depend upon the Holy Spirit to guide me throughout each day?

_____

_____

Something to Ponder

Do I trust that I am saved through the blood of Jesus
Christ and let the Holy Spirit guide and direct my path
daily? Is the fruit of the Spirit evident in my life?

PRAYER

Thank You, Lord, for loving me in spite of myself, for forgiving my
sins, and for guiding me in Your ways. Help me to be open to Your
leadership and focus on Your presence in my life daily.

Reflections

Use the space provided below to record your reflections on the lesson just completed. Think about the study and all the questions—including the personal application—and record anything that stood out, provided enlightenment, reduced your fears, or enriched your relationship with God.

CHAPTER 6

What Does a Christian Look Like?

But the fruit of the Spirit is love, joy, peace, longsuffering,
kindness, goodness, faithfulness, gentleness, self-control.
Against such there is no law.
Galatians 5:22–23

Doug's Story

Driving home from a deacons' meeting, Doug was fuming that the elders couldn't come to an agreement on the workshop he had been planning. *Why doesn't anyone see how much work I've put into this workshop on unity in the church? I have done more for this church than the pastor. In fact, I'm a better Christian than he is. He would never devote this much time to any project. I work harder than anyone in that church.*

At least I know I am doing all I can for the Lord. No one else seems to care about serving God. It's all about the show.

When Doug got home, he called out to his wife, Carolyn, "Hi, hon. Sorry I'm late. As usual, no one else wanted to get involved, so I have to do this workshop all by myself. I wish there were some true Christians in that church. I'm sure God would appreciate it too."

"Oh, don't be so hard on them. You have your own way of doing things. They are probably doing a lot more than you give them credit for. They just don't go at it the same way you do."

"You're just siding with them as you always do. You don't realize how much pressure I'm under because no one else wants to help with my projects."

"Since when is it your project? I thought it was God's."

Shrugging and resigned to anger, Doug walked into the bedroom. *I just can't talk to that woman. She never sees my side of anything.*

After a cooling-off period, Carolyn walked into their bedroom. "I'm sorry, honey. I've had a rough day too. One of the kids at school is having a tough time. Her dad just took all their money out of the bank and ran off with someone else. Her mom, who also goes to our church, can't seem to find a job. They have no money and are being evicted from their house. My student came to school without a lunch because the family can't even afford food. I feel like I should do something, but I don't know what."

"There's nothing you can do about it. Let the authorities know, and they will handle it."

"That's not what the Bible says to do. It says we are to care for others. Isn't there something we could do to help them out?"

"No. I don't have any extra money, and they're sure not staying here."

"Well, I think we should do something."

"Do what you think is right, but don't spend much money because I have plans to fix the patio, and we need all the extra money we can get our hands on for that."

Walking away, she said, "Whatever."

Carolyn thought about it and knelt down in prayer. *God, help me to see what it is You want me to do about this situation. I know I'm supposed to help in some way.*

Later, still debating what she should or could do to help them, she thought, *Zoey is such a sweet little girl, and her mother must be beside herself since she is unable to support her daughter right now. I've got to do something.*

I'll call the church tomorrow and see if they have any funds available to help with the rent. Maybe I could call social services to get some food stamps and money. I'll go through my closet to see if there is anything Zoey's mother might be able to wear that would make her more presentable for a job interview. Maybe I can help her with hair or makeup too. I could take some groceries over, and Doug wouldn't even have to know about it. I have lots of canned stuff in the garage, so the groceries might not cost that much and would help tide them over.

The next day Carolyn called their pastor to see if there was any way the church could help.

He seemed alarmed and said, "I'm surprised Doug didn't mention this to me this morning."

"Oh, he's too busy with this upcoming workshop to think about anything else right now."

"Well, let me see what we can do."

Later that day she called the social services office to find out if any help might be available for Zoey's mom, Debbie. "I'm just checking it out for a friend. Is there any possibility she might qualify for some help?"

The clerk was kind and said, "Well, I'd have to talk to Debbie and get a little more information. Do you think she could come by tomorrow around two?"

"I don't know. Can I call you back after I speak with her?"

"Yes, just let me know before five today."

Carolyn got out of the car at Debbie's house and knocked on the door. When Debbie opened it, Carolyn said, "Debbie, I need to talk to you. I just called social services, and they want to see you at two tomorrow to see if you qualify for some assistance. They might be able to pay the rent and give you some food stamps and maybe more. Are you in? Could you go if I took you?"

"Yes, absolutely. That would be great."

The next day they drove to the social services office and Marnie, the social worker, asked them to sit down. "I just need to get a little more information from you to see if you qualify. Could you fill out this form for me?"

"Sure," Debbie replied. Debbie completed the form and anxiously waited while Marnie reviewed the information on it.

"Well, it looks like we might be able to help you, but I'll need a few days to run it through the process. I should have an answer for you by next Tuesday."

"Thank you so much. Carolyn, I didn't know there might be help available. I have been in such a funk lately that I can't even think straight."

"Don't worry. God is on your side, and He will make sure that you are taken care of one way or another. He always does. By the way, I have some clothes here I thought you might like. They would be good for a job interview."

"Carolyn, why are you so good to me? I barely know you."

"Because God loves you, and so do I. We all need help at times, and our purpose here is to help each other in times of need."

When Carolyn arrived home, Doug was fuming. "Where have you been? I couldn't get hold of you all afternoon."

"I was helping Debbie. I took her to social services to see if she could get some financial aid."

"That's not your responsibility. I needed you to pick up the clothes from the cleaners and go to the bank for me. Debbie should be able to take care of herself. She's a grown woman."

"Doug, the woman was just dumped by her husband. He took all their money, and she has no job and a child to feed. Don't you think she could use a little help? Isn't it our responsibility to care for the needs of others too?"

"Hey, we tithe to the church and give to the Red Cross. I think we do our fair share."

"What has happened to you? You used to be a very loving, caring guy. Now all you talk about is what a great guy you are and what a spiritual leader you are. Somehow I'm not buying into that picture right now. You don't seem to care about anything or anyone but yourself and how you look to others. I love you, but I really don't like the way you are acting."

"Well, I don't like the way you're behaving either. You care more about others than you do me."

"That's not true! Just because I didn't run your errands today doesn't mean I don't take care of you. Your house is clean, your dinner is prepared every night, your clothes are washed, and I do my best to make you happy, which has been a hard thing to do lately.

"You say you are such a spiritual leader because you do so much for the church, but God doesn't want anyone to labor for the church if their heart isn't in the right place. Remember the greatest commandment? We are to love God first—not the church—and love others as ourselves. Is that what you're doing? God doesn't need you to do a bunch of work at the church. He wants you to want to serve Him by serving the church *and* others—not because it makes you look like a saintly person, but because you love Him first and foremost, and you love others and treat them the way you would like to be ministered to. That is the sign of true Christianity. What has happened to make you so insensitive?"

As he stormed his way into the bedroom, Doug shouted, "I give up! I'm going to bed! Good night."

Lying in bed, Doug thought about what Carolyn had said. He tossed and turned all night. *I am exhausted and stressed out, and for what? Maybe Carolyn is right and I have lost touch with God and myself. I got carried away with my workshop and forgot that it was to point people to Jesus. I haven't devoted much time to the family lately. I've been going through the motions at church so everyone would know what a great Christian leader I am, and I haven't been there for anyone in the past few months.*

Finally Doug came to realize how far he had fallen spiritually, and he cried out to God: *Father, please forgive me. I got carried away with my position and forgot it was about serving You. I've become hardened and inattentive to the needs of my family and others. I am sorry. I never meant to be that way. The stress and my ego just kind of snuck up on me. Please help me to change and get back to focusing on You.*

Bible Study: Galatians 6

This story illustrates many of the main points in Galatians 6, where it talks about what an abomination pride, arrogance, and judgmental attitudes are to God. Those traits are opposite to restoration of the fallen and forgiveness of others. It especially emphasizes that while Christian works are a good thing, they are not equivalent to a truly repentant person who loves and wants to serve God because they love Him.

GALATIANS 6:1–5

Paul tells believers that when someone has fallen into sin, we are to help restore them with a compassionate, forgiving spirit. Criticism does no good, but only serves to injure the person and make them less likely to want to turn back to a godly life.

When we see a Christian slip into sin—whether doing so knowingly or unaware of their wickedness—we are to help restore them to a right relationship with God. That does not mean we are to criticize or belittle them. It is our Christian responsibility to approach them in an empathetic, compassionate, and loving manner. We should never think we are more spiritual or better qualified to lead them, because the truth is, we all falter at times. If we believe ourselves better than others, we are looking toward our next failure.

> *When we see a Christian who has slipped into sin, we are to help restore them.*
> *Our approach should be nonjudgmental, empathetic, compassionate, and loving.*

Everyone goes through tough times, and we all have our own strengths and weaknesses. What derails our friend may not faze us at all, but in due time there will be something that throws us off track, which may have no impact on our friend. We are here to bolster and support each other in our quest for a godly life.

Think about yourself or your children. When you or they do wrong, do you try to justify or minimize it in your mind? Of course we all do, to some extent. No one wants to feel guilty, nor do they want their kids to be made out to be unruly. We look for the best in them. That is the way we should treat others, with love and compassion. Yes, we need to call them on their stuff, but it should be done in a gentle, compassionate manner to help restore them back to that right relationship with God.

If we presume we are Christian leaders who must bring others under submission to us, we are only fooling ourselves. We are no better than they are, and we should never compare ourselves to others. Everyone has a different pathway through life, and some get hit harder than others. We don't know what led them to the path they took; we don't know all the garbage in their background, so we don't really know where they are coming from, just as they don't know our history. Only God knows what they've been through and why they responded in the manner they did, and He loves them anyway. He doesn't condemn them, so why should we?

It is vital that we examine our own lives and ask God to show us the areas where we need to shape up. Are you arrogant, thinking yourself better than others? If so, then ask God to forgive and help you with that problem. In fact, we should ask God daily to reveal our shortcomings. God will speak to us if we take the time to stop and listen to Him.

Often we minimize or justify our own sins, thinking they are not that bad. However, we might feel much differently about it when we face God at the judgment. That little white lie may not be so little then. The less we worry about our small sins, the more we should worry about our sincerity in serving God. We are to serve God, not self. While we may think nothing of a slight indiscretion, a sin is still a sin. When we realize our sin, we need to ask forgiveness and turn from our wicked ways.

If we think we are better than others, we are only deceiving ourselves, and sooner or later we will suffer the consequences of our actions. Remember the story of the Pharisee who went to the temple to pray and thanked God that he was not like the others? Then the tax collector went to the temple to pray and ask for forgiveness (Luke 18:12–14). The tax man knew only God's grace could save him, and God heard his prayer and he was forgiven. Not so for the Pharisee. He was proud and arrogant and left without forgiveness for his sins. Is our condescension really worth the effort? God is the one who forgives our sins, and He will bring us down if we remain superior in our own minds.

> *The less we worry about our small sins, the more we should worry about our sincerity in serving God.*

Our arrogance is more likely to make another sinner dig their heels in and walk away. We will not gain respect for our attitude or helpfulness, and our arrogance is a total turnoff. It does nothing good for the sinner or for us. God hates a proud spirit, and we will pay for our transgression of arrogance.

Aside from restoring someone who has yielded to sin, we are also called to meet the needs of others. Everyone gets hit with problems. Some are small and some are devastating catastrophes. Our job is to meet the needs of others. We are to help everyone, but we should place a priority on others in the Christian community.

I have a friend who was sick, and I asked if I could bring her meals. She declined (as most of us would unless we were in dire straits). Later I found out she had been subsisting on canned chicken noodle soup. She was out of crackers and bread and quite a few other essentials. I now realize I should have just taken her some food since I knew she was bedridden. I should not have asked, because many of us are too proud to accept help when offered, even if it would be a godsend. I have resolved now to take food to people I know could use a meal, even if they say they don't need it.

Food is not the only way we can help, though. People may need a ride to the doctor, or they may need someone to clean their house, do miscellaneous chores, offer financial aid, or maybe just spend time talking and praying with them. It is our responsibility to be there for them.

The most significant command is: "'And you shall love the Lord your God with all your heart, with all your soul, with all your mind, and with all your strength.' This is the first commandment. And the second, like it, is this: 'You shall love your neighbor as yourself'" (Mark 20:30–31).

Galatians 6:6–11

People minimize their lousy behavior, thinking things like, *It was just a little white lie* or *God will understand why I hate that guy's guts. After all, he ruined my life.* But a sin is a sin no matter what we've done. We will be held accountable for every wrong thing we've done when we face God. We should not be so flippant when it comes to sin.

Unsaved people like to think they will get to heaven because, *After all, I am a good person.* No, that won't cut it! God says to accept Jesus Christ as our Lord and Savior, confess our sins, and turn from them. Will we ever be perfect? No! But we are to ask God to help us learn to trust and follow Him as well as set the example of a godly life for others.

Some may profess Christianity and even go to church regularly, but that is the extent of their faith. Others attend church often and possibly even go to Bible study or get involved in church leadership roles. They profess Christianity to others, but there is no real change in their hearts. They want others to think they are Christian because it makes them look good. That's pretty much what the Pharisees did, and God wasn't happy with them either.

God knows our hearts and cannot be deceived. Our time here on earth is precious in the sight of the Lord, and we are accountable for our actions. God will not be mocked. Our purpose is to praise and glorify God and lead others to Christ through our godly example. That does not mean we need to stand on the street corner and yell things like "You must be saved!" or quote John 3:16. While those may be good things to do for some, what God is looking for is a willing heart to do whatever He directs us to do. It may be as simple as showing up with a meal when someone is sick or paying someone's rent when they are down and out.

Anyone who lives selfishly and ignores the needs of others is ignoring God and will have nothing good to show for his life. Living in the flesh (world) includes attempting to gain salvation by works, but works cannot save us. Fleshly living also includes sin of any kind, including conceit. Our calling is to do good, and in that, we are charged with meeting the needs of others. It is good to get involved in social justice, but our priority should be helping those in the Christian community first.

Pastors especially need our support, and they are entitled to it. Pastors should receive adequate compensation and help in any other manner required. It is crucial that we tithe to support our church and our pastors. Stinginess in giving is like mocking God. God is our provider, and it is only by His grace that we have money in the first place. If we devote our resources to satisfying ourselves rather than asking God for direction for our finances, we will eventually receive what is due us. If we try to keep our resources to ourselves, we could wind up losing it all. Remember how God was more grateful for the widow's mite (Luke 21:1–4) than for the money the Pharisee put in the collection plate? God sees all and compensates accordingly.

When we live a godly life, we don't worry so much about our salvation because we are assured of it. We have faith to know that God is intimately involved in every aspect of our lives and we can go to Him twenty-four hours a day (He has indwelled us with His Holy Spirit). He is always here to guide and direct our paths, to provide our needs, and to comfort and encourage us.

When we try to help others, we can feel overwhelmed. So many people need so much, and we have busy schedules, limited resources, and so on. Watch and guard against this thinking. God promises rewards for perseverance in doing good deeds. We should strive to do good in our lifetime, and we should make this the first order of business in our lives. When new needs appear, as much as we are able we should work for the benefit of all, starting with the family of God.

Galatians 6:12–15

Paul is reminding the Galatians that circumcision can be just an act of the flesh, just as the other laws were that the Jewish leaders were trying to make them follow. Those justifications are not of the Spirit. The religious leaders weren't even adhering to all the laws themselves. They just wanted to impose them on others to elevate their own positions in the church. The Pharisees looked and acted like pious leaders of the temple, which afforded them power and reverence from the people.

Some people will work hard in the ministry only to boast of what they have done. "Look at what I've done for the Lord," they may say. That is prideful and an abomination to God. God doesn't need us to do anything for Him; He can accomplish all by Himself. We are called to serve because we love Him and want to bring others to know Him—not because He needs us to, but because we love Him and we love others. It is not going to enhance our position in the heavenly realm or make us more important here on earth. Our purpose is to serve God and glorify Him for who He is and because of what Jesus did for us.

> *God doesn't need us to do anything for Him. He is perfectly capable of accomplishing all things by Himself. We are called to serve because we love Him and want to bring others to know Him.*

Our vanity and sinful nature make us want to be admired by others. To obtain the accolades, we do all kinds of good works and make sure everyone knows about it. That is not the spirit of true Christianity, but instead is considered works of the flesh. We often fail to realize that it is only by God's grace that we are able to do anything and that we need to give God the glory.

We should never worry about what the world thinks of us. The more we realize the suffering Christ endured for us, the more we understand that we have no right to brag about anything. Our sole purpose in doing good works is to glorify God for what He has done.

> *We often fail to realize it is only by God's grace that we are able to do anything. It is God who enables us, and He deserves all the glory for our accomplishments.*

It is easy to look at the lives of the rich and famous and think they have it all. But behind closed doors, many of those affluent, influential people are utterly miserable. You can have power and money affording you the opportunity to do anything you like, but if you have no peace within, you are still unhappy.

The peace God gives surpasses all worldly treasures. When you consider that God really loves you and values you as a person, that He will meet all your needs and cares about your provisions and happiness, what more do you really want?

This world offers many things, but without God they mean nothing. What we desire more than anything is inner peace and love. These are only attainable through living godly lives. Once we become Christians, our whole value system changes. We no longer need friendship with the world with all its backbiting, chaos, and worry. We have peace within and are content to lean on God and serve Him. Our new spirit changes our disposition and causes us to have faith that God will protect, provide, and guide our path by faith working through love.

While works cannot justify or save us, they are still an essential part of the life of faith God planned for all believers. We were put here with a purpose. How else will we reach the lost for Christ?

Paul reminds the believers of the torture and suffering he endured, as evidenced by the marks on his body. This was not to elevate himself in their eyes, but to demonstrate his authenticity—he was all in when it came to serving Christ. Perhaps mentioning all he had gone through was alluding to the Galatians' lack of sincerity.

True believers have changed mindsets and hearts. God enables us to believe in the Lord Jesus and to live godly lives. We cannot fake it without sooner or later being found out. Only true Christianity will stand the test of time. God is our ultimate judge, but the world recognizes the real deal and is impacted by it. When someone living in the flesh goes through a catastrophe, who do they turn to? A Christian who has demonstrated a godly life to them!

GALATIANS 6:16–18

Our new creation is in the image of Christ. Faith is the most significant distinction between Christians and others. God blesses all who walk by faith. Peace and a clear conscience are part of the package.

God provides everything we need, is merciful to us, and showers us with many other blessings when we trust in Him. The Bible is our ultimate rulebook, both in its doctrines and precepts. Let us not be swayed by what men say unless the message is backed by the Bible.

Although Paul had experienced extreme torture and many other sufferings, he still talked to the Galatians in humility, with tender affection for them. Paul stresses that this happiness is not dependent upon religious rules or works. God indwells our hearts and spirits, comforting and strengthening us. All we need to be content is the grace of our Lord Jesus Christ.

Study Questions

GALATIANS 6:1–5

What are we to do when a Christian brother or sister falls into sin? (v. 1)

_____

_____

What must we guard against when trying to restore others?

_____

_____

What steps should be taken in restoring someone to Christ?
   √   Gal. 6:1–4
   √   2 Cor. 5:18

_____

_____

Whose life are we to examine? (Ps. 19:12; 139:23)

_____

_____

Should we compare ourselves to others? Why or why not?

_____

_____

If we are to bear others' burdens, how might we accomplish that?

_____

When should we be willing to help others? Only when it is convenient?

_____

_____

GALATIANS 6:6–11

What is the commitment we are asked to give when we accept Jesus Christ as our Lord and Savior? (John 14:21)

_____

_____

What does Paul say we shall reap by living this way?

_____

_____

Are we to discriminate when deciding who to help?

_____

_____

Who should we help first?

_____

_____

How can we demonstrate God's love to nonbelievers if we only help fellow believers, family, or friends?

_____

_____

GALATIANS 6:12–15

Do some people spread the gospel while unwittingly sinning? (Proverbs 21:24)

_____

_____

Why can't we live a righteous life all the time? (Rom. 3:23–24)

_____

_____

The Bible says we shall reap what we sow. Does that mean that, since we are Christians, we will have a great life here on earth?

_____

_____

How was Paul affected by the objects or people around him?

_____

_____

How can Christians living out their faith avoid getting too caught up in the things of this world? (Heb. 12:2; Matt. 22:37)

_____

_____

What demonstrates a changed heart in the lives of believers? (Gal. 5:22–23)

_____

_____

GALATIANS 6:16–18

What is the greatest distinction between Christians and nonbelievers?

_____

_____

What blessings may a Christian expect?

_____

_____

What was Paul's prayer for the believers?

_____

_____

Personal Application

How does my walk reflect my talk? (Gal. 6:7)

_____

_____

Am I really living out my faith and trusting God for the consequences?

_____

_____

Am I spreading the Word and showing love to others because I genuinely care about their welfare, or am I performing to look righteous before others?

_____

_____

Am I being stingy with my resources, or am I giving unto God to support His ministry?

_____

_____

Do I have a tendency to judge or criticize others?

_____

_____

Something to Ponder

Am I living my life in such a way that people will see
God's love flowing through me to others?
Is my motivation to love and serve God or to
impress others with my "holy" lifestyle?

PRAYER

Thank You, Lord, for Your loving presence and provisions in my life. Help me to extend that love to everyone I come in contact with. Help me also to have empathy and care for others who are in need, pointing them to Your love for them.

Reflections

Use the space provided below to record your reflections on the lesson just completed. Think about the study and all the questions—including the personal application—and record anything that stood out, provided enlightenment, reduced your fears, or enriched your relationship with God.

Order Information

To order additional copies of this book, please visit
www.redemption-press.com.
Also available on Amazon.com and BarnesandNoble.com
Or by calling toll-free 1-844-2REDEEM.